DISNEY · PIXAR

# FINDING NEMO

## All About SHARKS
### From Tooth to Tail

by Adrienne Mason

Scholastic Inc.

New York · Toronto · London · Auckland · Sydney
Mexico City · New Delhi · Hong Kong · Buenos Aires

Cover Designer: Aruna Goldstein
Designer: Julia Sarno
Interior illustrations: Yancey Labat

Photos:
Pages 6-7: (background: Seascape Batfish school silhouette sun & surface waves) © Robert Yin / SeaPics.com.
Pages 8-9: (background: Full-frame underwater view of very heavy tropical rain on sea surface) © Kim Westerskov /Stone/Getty Images.
Pages 10-11: (background: Lagoon Shallow, underwater view) © Pete Atkinson /The Image Bank/ Getty Images.
Page 10: (shark denticles) © Will Schubert / SeaPics.com.
Pages 12-13: (background-underwater at NELHA, Natural Energy Lab Hawaii, Big Island, Pacific) © David Kearnes / SeaPics.com.
Page 13: (nurse shark) © Masa Ushioda / SeaPics.com.
Pages 14-15: (background: sunlight shining through sea water, underwater view Vava'u Islands, Tonga, Polynesia) © Darryl Torckler/ Photographer's Choice/ Getty Images.
Page 14: (great white shark) © Tim Davis/Corbis; (carpet shark) © Doug Perrine / SeaPics.com.
Page 15: (swell shark) © Mark Conlin / SeaPics.com; (thresher shark) © Doug Perrine /SeaPics.com; (cookie cutter shark) © Gwen Lowe / SeaPics.com;
    (dolphin) © Michael S. Nolan / SeaPics.com.
Pages 16-17: (background: Lagoon Shallow, underwater view) © Pete Atkinson /The Image Bank/ Getty Images.
Page 16: (hammerhead shark) © Doug Perrine / SeaPics.com; (basking shark) © Dan Burton / SeaPics.com; (goblin shark) © David Shen / SeaPics.com.
Page 17: (spiny dogfish) © Doug Perrine / SeaPics.com; (tiger shark) © David B. Fleetham / SeaPics.com; (mako shark) © Jeremy Stafford-Deitsch / SeaPics.com.
Page 19: (puzzle background) Water Reflection in the Red Sea) © Ian Cartwright/ Photodisc Green (RF)/Getty Images.
Page 20: (leopard shark) © Michael Aw/ Photodisc Green (RF) /Getty Images.
Page 21: (horn shark) © Tom Campbell / SeaPics.com; (kelp forest) © Brandon D. Cole/Corbis; (white-tip reef shark) © Stephen Frink/ Digital Vision (RF)/Getty Images;
    (whale shark) © Brain J Skerry / National Geographic/Getty Images.
Page 22: (pygmy shark) © Masa Ushioda / SeaPics.com; (angel shark) © Rudie Kuiter / SeaPics.com; (blue shark) © Bill Curtsinger/ National Geographic/Getty Images.
Page 23: (background:Yellow-stripe goatfish or Mulloidichthys vanicolensis) © image100 (RF)/ Getty Images; (shark eye) © Jeff Rotman / SeaPics.com.
Page 24: (background:Yellow-stripe goatfish or Mulloidichthys vanicolensis) © image100 (RF)/ Getty Images; (leopard shark) © Doug Perrine / SeaPics.com;
    (nose of gray reef shark) © Jonathan Bird /  SeaPics.com.
Page 25: (background: Purple anthias fish and a canoe overhead, Papua New Guinea) © Altrendo Nature / Getty Images; (great white shark) © Cousteau Society/ The Image Bank/
    Getty Images, (great white shark tooth) © Doc White / SeaPics.com.
Pages 26-27: (background:Purple anthias fish and a canoe overhead, Papua New Guinea) © Altrendo Nature / Getty Images.
Page 26: (Port Jackson shark) © Jeffrey L. Rotman/Corbis; (lemon shark) © Steve Drogin / SeaPics.com; (nurse shark) © Masa Ushioda / SeaPics.com.
Page 27: (whale shark) © Tom Haight / SeaPics.com; (megalodon jaws) © Jeff Rotman / SeaPics.com.
Pages 28-29: (background: rippled water, full frame, underwater view) © Ken Usami/ Photodisc Red (RF)/ Getty Images.
Page 28: (striped catshark egg case) © Doug Perrine / SeaPics.com; (horn shark egg case) © Marty Snyderman / SeaPics.com; (swell shark egg case) © Michele Hall / SeaPics.com;
    (swell shark embryo) © Howard Hall / SeaPics.com.
Page 29: (baby swell shark) © Mark Conlin / SeaPics.com.
Page 30: (background: rippled water, full frame, underwater view) © Ken Usami/ Photodisc Red (RF)/ Getty Images; (lemon shark and pups) © Doug Perrine / SeaPics.com;
    (scalloped hammerhead shark pups) © Andre Seale / SeaPics.com.
Page 31: (background: light patterns on shallow seabed, underwater view) © Darryl Torckler/ Photographer's Choice/ Getty Images.
Page 32: (background: light patterns on shallow seabed, underwater view) © Darryl Torckler/ Photographer's Choice/ Getty Images.
Page 33: (Caribbean reef shark) © Doug Perrine / SeaPics.com; (shark tag) © Doug Perrine / SeaPics.com.
Page 34: (divers with black-tip reef shark) © Doug Perrine / SeaPics.com; (divers in cage) © Masa Ushioda / SeaPics.com.
Page 36: (leopard shark) © Aaron Carlisle, MLML /Getty Images; (smooth hound shark) © David B. Fleetham / SeaPics.com.
Page 37: (background: Water Reflection in the Red Sea) © Ian Cartwright/ Photodisc Green (RF)/Getty Images.

Published by Scholastic Inc., 557 Broadway, New York, NY 10012, by arrangement
with Disney Licensed Publishing. SCHOLASTIC, UNDERSEA SCHOOL, and
associated logos are trademarks and/or registered trademarks of Scholastic Inc.

ISBN 0-439-80884-7

12 11 10 9 8 7 6 5 4 3 2 1     5 6 7 8 9 10/0

Printed in the U.S.A.
First Scholastic printing, August 2005

# Table of Contents

**Nemo**
*clown fish*

# Let's Swim with the SHARKS!

**H**I! It's me, Nemo! It's nice to "sea" you again! On this underwater adventure we're going to hang out with some of my favorite fish in the sea—sharks! Don't be frightened, though. There are so many cool things to learn about sharks you won't have time to be scared. Did you know that there are more than 375 kinds of sharks in the sea? Sharks can be smaller than a baseball bat or larger than a bus, but only a few kinds have ever harmed people. In this book you'll:

- **meet a shark with a mouth like a cookie cutter.**

- **find out why sharks have rows and rows of teeth.**

- **learn about a shark's super senses.**

- **discover sharks that glow to attract prey!**

**Anchor**
*hammerhead shark*

**Bruce**
*great white shark*

**Chum**
*mako shark*

Sharks like Bruce, Chum, and Anchor are some of the best hunters in the sea. Almost all sharks are predators. This means they hunt and eat other animals, mostly fish. Sharks are a type of fish, just like me, Dory, and Tad. But sharks are called cartilaginous (car-tuh-LAH-jin-uhs) fish. Instead of having bones in their body, they have skeletons made of flexible and rubbery stuff called cartilage. There are lots of other special things about sharks. Are you ready to find out what it takes to be a shark?
Let's go!

I'm glad that I'm Bruce's friend and not his food. Uh, at least I think I am. Right, Bruce?

**Dory**
*blue tang*

# Chapter 1: Shark Parts

The smallest shark in the world, the dwarf dogfish, is only about eight inches (20 cm) long. It would easily fit inside a shoebox! The whale shark is the largest kind of shark. It can be as long as ten park benches, lined up end to end. (The whale shark is also the biggest fish in the world.) Big or small, all sharks share the same kind of body. Let's take a peek at the parts of a shark.

## The Shape of a Hunter

Most sharks are built for speed. They have a pointy snout and their bodies are narrower near their tail. With this sleek, streamlined shape, sharks can slip through the water easily as they chase their food, or prey.

### Skin

Never snuggle with a shark. Their skin is like sandpaper. Ouch! Sharkskin is covered with tiny tooth-like growths, called denticles. Old denticles are always being replaced by new, slightly larger, denticles.

### Caudal (Tail) Fin

The shark swishes its caudal fin from side to side to swim forward.

### Pelvic Fins

Like the dorsal fins, these keep the shark straight in the water.

**Dorsal Fin**

This fin keeps the shark straight in the water and prevents it from rolling over. The dorsal fin sometimes sticks up above the water's surface. Some sharks have two dorsal fins.

**Teeth**

Sharks keep the tooth fairy working overtime! Sharks have lots of razor-sharp teeth that are arranged in rows. When a tooth breaks off or falls out, a new, sharp tooth is ready to take its place. During its lifetime, a shark can replace thousands of teeth.

**Pectoral Fins**

A shark holds these fins out from the sides of its body. They help the shark move up or down in the water. A shark can tilt these fins slightly to help it slow down.

**Gill Slits**

Water flows in through a shark's mouth and out through five, six, or seven gill slits. That is how fish "breathe." You can read more about this on page 13.

11

# The Inside Scoop on Sharks

Blood, guts, muscles, and more...that's what's inside a shark. Like all animals, sharks have a brain, heart, stomach, intestines, and other organs. But they have some parts that are different, too.

## Brain

A shark's brain controls all of a shark's actions, just like how your brain controls your actions. A lot of a shark's brain is used for its senses, including smell and sight. You'll learn more about a shark's super senses on pages 23 and 24.

## Vertebral Column

A shark's backbone extends into the top part of its tail fin. This stiff fin helps sharks speed through the water!

## Liver

A shark's liver is filled with oil. Oil is lighter than water, so a shark's large liver helps it stay afloat.

## Gills

Sharks use blood-filled gills to absorb oxygen out of the water.

## Shark Cousins

Sharks are closely related to other fish that have skeletons made of cartilage. Rays, skates, guitarfish, and sawfish are all cartilaginous fish, too. Most of these fish live close to the ocean floor, where they feed on fish, worms, and shellfish, like clams.

## Breathing like a shark

Like all fish, sharks get the oxygen they need from the water. Water flows in through their mouth, across their gills, and out through five to seven gill slits. Blood in their gills draws oxygen out of the water.

Sharks that live on the ocean floor, like nurse sharks, bring water to their gills through holes on the top of their head. This way, their gills aren't clogged with sand or mud.

nurse shark

### CLOWNING AROUND!

**Q:** How do you make a shark float?

**A:** With two scoops of ice cream, a big bottle of soda, and a shark!

marlin
*clown fish*

## Hot Blood or Cold?

Most fish, and most sharks, have blood that is the same temperature as the water around them. So, if the water is cold, their blood is cold. Five kinds of sharks, including great white sharks, like Bruce, have warm blood like you do. These fast-swimming sharks hold onto some of the heat produced by their powerful muscles.

13

# Chapter 2: Sharks of the World

Sharks are named after some pretty odd things...like goblins, carpets, tigers, angels, and dogs. Are you ready to meet a few of my shark friends? Hey, Bruce! Let's start with you. Tell us about great white sharks!

## The Shape of a Hunter

I might not eat meat, but all of the other great white sharks in the world do. Great white sharks are powerful predators. They are some of the largest and most fearsome sharks in the sea. Great white sharks can swim in fast bursts of speed. Sometimes they come completely out of the water!

*great white shark*

*carpet shark*

Carpet sharks lie on the ocean bottom just like a carpet lies on your floor! Carpet sharks and angel sharks hide on the sand waiting for fish, crabs, or snails to come within chomping distance.

## Breathing like a shark

Like all fish, sharks get the oxygen they need from the water. Water flows in through their mouth, across their gills, and out through five to seven gill slits. Blood in their gills draws oxygen out of the water.

Sharks that live on the ocean floor, like nurse sharks, bring water to their gills through holes on the top of their head. This way, their gills aren't clogged with sand or mud.

nurse shark

### CLOWNING AROUND!

**Q:** How do you make a shark float?

**A:** With two scoops of ice cream, a big bottle of soda, and a shark!

**marlin**
*clown fish*

## Hot Blood or Cold?

Most fish, and most sharks, have blood that is the same temperature as the water around them. So, if the water is cold, their blood is cold. Five kinds of sharks, including great white sharks, like Bruce, have warm blood like you do. These fast-swimming sharks hold onto some of the heat produced by their powerful muscles.

# Chapter 2: Sharks of the World

Sharks are named after some pretty odd things...like goblins, carpets, tigers, angels, and dogs. Are you ready to meet a few of my shark friends? Hey, Bruce! Let's start with you. Tell us about great white sharks!

## The Shape of a Hunter

I might not eat meat, but all of the other great white sharks in the world do. Great white sharks are powerful predators. They are some of the largest and most fearsome sharks in the sea. Great white sharks can swim in fast bursts of speed. Sometimes they come completely out of the water!

great white shark

Carpet sharks lie on the ocean bottom just like a carpet lies on your floor! Carpet sharks and angel sharks hide on the sand waiting for fish, crabs, or snails to come within chomping distance.

carpet shark

14

*spiny dogfish*

Spiny dogfish are small sharks that usually roam in packs, just like dogs sometimes do. They can travel in groups of hundreds or even thousands. Spiny dogfish eat anything they can nab with their strong jaws and teeth—including shrimp and large fish.

Tiger sharks are not picky eaters. They chow down on turtles, birds, other sharks, fish, dolphins...pretty much anything in the sea. But they don't stop at live food. They eat junk too! Bottles, bicycle parts, boots, and even a raincoat have been found in their stomachs!

*tiger shark*

Mako sharks, like me, are sleek, like a fast sports car. We're built for speed and are the fastest sharks in the world! We even leap out of the water as we chase our food, which includes fast-swimming fish like swordfish, tuna, and even other sharks.

*mako shark*

## CLOWNING AROUND!

**Q:** How does a dogfish's skin feel?

**A:** Rough, rough!

# Shark Chart: Super Big and Super Small

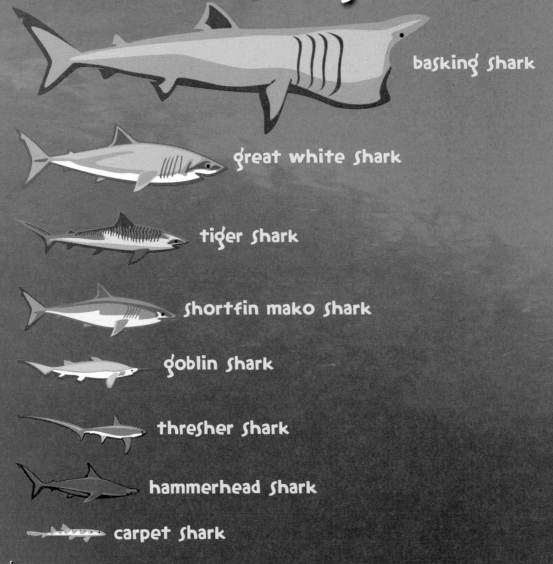

basking shark

great white shark

tiger shark

shortfin mako shark

goblin shark

thresher shark

hammerhead shark

carpet shark

So, you can see that not all sharks are big and scary and mean. We've got lots more to learn about sharks, but first, let's take a break and play a Fishy Fun game.

# FISHY FUN: Searching for Sharks

You've met lots of sharks already—but there are many more sharks in the ocean, just waiting to be discovered! There are 15 names of sharks hidden in this word search. Can you find all of the shark names in the yellow box below? The names can go down, sideways, or diagonally. Good luck!
*(When you're done with your search, turn to page 38.)*

angel
bamboo
bullhead
carpet
crocodile
finetooth
gulper
lantern
mud
prickly
saw
sleeper
slime
swell
tiger

```
H C R C T I G E R K E T
O T B C A B S W M S E B
B T U A R R A T B W H A
E O L R R E P M D H P D
N O L P E I L E B T B E
T C H A P S S C T O T C
E R E L M E A D W N O R
E O A R G U B S W E L L
P C D N I L D E B L I L
R O A F I N E T O O T H
I D S G U L P E R W T M
C I G U K P E A A N O P
K L A N G E L S R L A T
L E K L A N T E R N E B
Y C H S L E E P E R R C
M S L I M E B U L L H A
E M R W D E I R C C B R
```

19

# Chapter 3: Home for a Shark

Sharks live in all of the world's oceans, from the frigid waters of the Arctic and Antarctic, to the sunlit, shallow waters near coral reefs. Let's take a closer look at some of the places that sharks call home sweet home.

## Sharks in the Grass

Leopard sharks slink throughout the shallows of *sloughs* (SLEWS). In the channels of the slough they find lots of food, like crabs, worms, and small fish. They also find great places to hide from larger sharks!

leopard shark

## That's a Mouthful, Mate!

A *slough* is a shallow area of land right next to the ocean. It's filled with narrow, winding channels of water, lots of grass-like plants, and mud.

# Forests in the sea

Did you know that there are forests in the ocean? They're filled with large seaweeds, called kelp. Many of the sharks that live in the kelp forests are slow-moving. The horn shark hides at the bottom of the kelp forest during the day and comes out to feed on clams and other shellfish at night.

horn shark

kelp forest

# Reef Roamer

white-tip reef shark

Many sharks, like this white-tip reef shark, hang out near coral reefs, where they feed on smaller fish. Some sharks hide in the nooks and crannies in the reef, waiting for prey to swim by.

# Giant cruisers

The whale shark cruises slowly through the ocean like a huge underwater blimp. It lives in warmer waters and usually travels near the surface, straining food as it swims.

whale shark

## CLOWNING AROUND!

**Q:** What did the baby horn shark say when it got lost in the ocean forest?

**A:** Kelp, kelp!

# Deep Dwellers

This tiny pygmy shark lives in the coldest, darkest, and deepest parts of the oceans. To attract prey and mates, it gives off a glow from a light in its belly.

pygmy shark

angel shark

Angel sharks are flat like a pancake. Their extra-large side fins look something like angel wings (or what angel wings might look like)! Their sandy-colored skin helps them hide in the sand on the ocean floor.

# On the Move

Some sharks don't stay in one place—they migrate, or swim over large distances. Blue sharks can travel across the Atlantic Ocean—from the east coast of the United States to Africa and back again. Many different sharks move as water temperatures change throughout the year. Most are following their food. Great white sharks travel the world's coastlines in search of food, like seals, fish, and seabirds.

blue shark

Did you ever wonder how sharks find their food or travel the world's oceans? They can't call for takeout, and they don't carry a map. But they can use their super senses! Ready to find out more? Just keep swimming along with me!

# Chapter 4: Super Sniffers and Extra-Special Eyes!

Sharks have incredible ways of seeing, smelling, tasting, and even feeling their way through their watery world. Their sharp senses help make them some of the best hunters in the sea.

## Sniffing Around

Sharks are super sniffers! They have a very keen sense of smell and can pick up the scents of fish and other animals in the water. They'd be able to detect a drop of blood in a large swimming pool!

I wonder if sharks could detect a drop of ink in a very large ocean!

**Pearl**
*octopus*

## Seeing is Believing

**Eye of a Caribbean reef shark**

Sharks have large eyes that help them see underwater. They also have a mirror-like surface on the back of their eyes. This "mirror" reflects light back into their eyes. All of this light helps sharks see well, even in the dark, deep sea.

Can you wink? Most fish can't because they don't have eyelids. But some sharks do have special eyelids that slide across their eyeballs. The eyelids protect their eyes when they attack prey.

## Feel But Don't Touch

Sharks can feel other fish in the water without even touching them. On the sides of their bodies, they have special liquid-filled tubes called lateral lines. These lateral lines help them "feel" from a distance. Tiny hairs in the tube sense any motion in the water. This way, the sharks can "feel" when anything—like dinner—happens to swim by!

leopard shark

lateral line

## It's Electric!

nose of a gray reef shark

A shark's nose is covered in tiny pits or pores. These jelly-filled pits are connected to the nerves under the shark's skin. All living things give off small electric signals. Sharks use their special "pits" to feel these signals. It's similar to how you can feel the heat from a lamp without touching it.

When hammerheads and other sharks swim, they swing their head from side to side. By doing this, they're using all of their special senses to search for food above and below the sand. It's similar to how someone uses a metal detector to find coins hidden under the sand.

Now you know some ways sharks find food! But just what are they looking for and how do they catch it? Let's find out!

# Chapter 5: Shark Bait

Sharks are predators on the prowl. They use their super senses to find their prey. But most sharks just don't gulp down anything that swims. They're pretty picky when it comes to deciding what's on the menu.

## chew on this

After sharks grab their prey and tear off a chunk, they swallow the pieces whole without chewing. Sharks can get some pretty big food inside their bellies. One great white shark was found with a shark almost half its size in its belly!

*Don't forget to chew, don't forget to chew… chewing, chewing…*

## Got a spare tooth or two?

*great white shark*

It's no big deal when a shark loses a tooth. They have lots of spares waiting to move in to replace it. Some sharks lose one tooth at a time, but sharks like spiny dogfish replace an entire row of teeth at once! Sharks' teeth come in many shapes and sizes.

*great white shark tooth*

Unlike most sharks, great white sharks use their strong, triangle-shaped teeth to chew their prey— usually seals, sea lions, other large fish (including sharks!), and sometimes dolphins

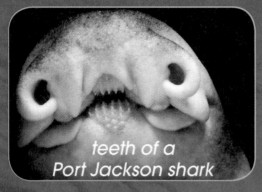

teeth of a
Port Jackson shark

Many sharks have teeth that are like tiny spikes, which they use for gripping smaller prey. The Port Jackson shark also has some flat teeth to crunch spiky sea urchins or hard-shelled mussels.

Rows of long, curved teeth, like those of a lemon shark are perfect for snagging fish, including spiky fish like porcupine fish or stingrays.

lemon shark

# slowly slurping sharks

Slow-moving nurse sharks aren't interested in chasing fast-moving prey. Instead, they eat crabs, shrimps, octopuses, snails, and other small prey. Sometimes they catch their food by using their strong lips to suck prey out of holes or cracks in rocks.

nurse shark

## CLOWNING AROUND!

**Q:** Where does a lemon shark go for help?

**A:** The lemon-*aid* stand!

# Gigantic Jaws

A shark's mouth is on the underside of its body. To bite their prey, sharks lift their snouts up and thrust their jaws out. This moves their sharp teeth forward as they chomp down. Sharks have very powerful jaws. Some large sharks have put holes in boats!

## Eating with Your Mouth Open

Whale sharks, basking sharks, and the bizarre megamouth sharks are some of the world's largest fish, but they have the tiniest teeth. They don't use these teeth to catch food. Instead, they use them to strain small food like shrimp, fish, fish eggs, and other floating creatures out of the water.

whale shark

## Open Wide!

Great white sharks are some of the world's largest and scariest sharks. But just imagine a shark three times longer and 20 times heavier! That is how large the megalodon might have been. This shark no longer exists, but its teeth have been found. One of the largest teeth was almost as tall as this page!

jaws of a megalodon shark

### CLOWNING AROUND!

**Q:** What's a shark's favorite meal?

**A:** Fish and *ships*!

27

# Chapter 6: Shark Babies

Dogs aren't the only animals that give birth to pups. Shark babies are called pups, too. There are a few different ways that pups can be born. Let's take a look into a shark's nursery.

## Shark Eggs

striped catshark egg case

horn shark egg case

Some sharks, like horn sharks and dogfish, lay eggs, sort of like hens do! The eggs are packed inside leathery egg cases (like a shell), with one egg in each case. Some egg cases have strings on the end, which catch on rocks or seaweeds on the ocean floor. Other egg cases are shaped in a way that they can be wedged into spaces between rocks. Shark parents don't take care of their eggs or their babies. The mother lays the egg case and then swims away.

swell shark egg case

For several months, the tiny pups develop inside the egg case. They are attached to a large egg sac filled with yolk. (It's something like the yolk you see in a chicken's egg.) The pups get the *nutrients* they need to grow from the yolk.

swell shark egg case with embryo

baby swell shark emerging from its egg case

When the pup has used up all of the egg sac, one end of the case comes apart and the baby shark swims out!

Newly hatched pups are shaped just like their parents—they're just smaller. Soon after hatching, they start to feed on small food, like small fish or shrimp. It will be years before they have babies of their own.

Tad
butterfly fish

Hey, these pups will be the new Undersea School students soon!

# That's a Mouthful, Mate!

Your food is full of *nutrients* (NEW-tree-ints). You need nutrients to grow healthy and strong. After you eat your lunch, the nutrients from the food are absorbed into your blood. A baby shark absorbs nutrients from its yolk sac or from its mother's blood.

# A Shark is Born!

Sharks are different from almost all of the other fish in the world because most of them, including lemon sharks and blue sharks, give birth to live babies. Shark mothers can have several babies growing inside them. These pups develop in eggs and hatch while they're still inside their mother. Eventually, they're born as live baby sharks.

*lemon shark giving birth to a live pup*

*scalloped hammerhead shark pups*

Shark pups, such as the hammerheads to the left, develop in a way that is similar to how you grew inside your mother! Instead of getting nutrients from an egg, these young sharks are connected to their mother by a special cord. They absorb the nutrients they need to grow from their mother's blood.

## Movin' Out

Shark pups are small so they need to stay hidden from predators. Many stay in shallow water where there are seaweeds, rocks, and caves to hide in. As they grow, they spend more and more time farther out at sea.

# Chapter 7: Shark Stories

People love to tell shark stories. Some of these stories are true, but many are not. Did you think that all sharks were mean eating machines? Now that you've met a few different sharks, you can see that sharks come in all shapes and sizes. Sure, they're predators, but all animals need to eat to survive. There are lots of stories, or myths, about sharks that aren't quite true. Bruce, Chum, and Anchor are going to give us the truthful scoop about these shark tales.

## Myth #1:
## Sharks Have No Enemies

Not quite, mate! Some sharks eat other sharks, but the biggest threat sharks have is humans. Yup, thirty to one-hundred million sharks are killed each year by people. Many of these sharks are caught for food or for their fins. Some are caught accidentally in fishing nets meant for other fish.

## Myth #2:
## All Sharks Are Dangerous to People

Out of 375 kinds of sharks, only a few types have ever attacked people. While shark attacks occur sometimes, dogs, bees, elephants, falling soda machines, lightning, and cars hurt more people every year than sharks do. So, by the look of things, sharks should be more afraid of humans than they are of them!

## Myth #3: Sharks Are Dumb

It's hard for scientists to measure intelligence, but studies with lemon sharks show that they learn faster than cats or rabbits. And, remember, sharks are predators. They have to use their incredible senses and brains to find, chase, and catch their prey.

## Myth #4: Sharks Aren't Important to the Ocean

Blimey! That's not right at all! All sea creatures have a place in the ocean. Sharks are predators. They keep populations of fish and other creatures in the ocean from growing too large. Many sharks also eat dead animals, so they are like the ocean cleanup crew.

Nice swimming, so far! Now that you know all about some shark tales, let's learn about people who work very hard to discover shark truths!

# Chapter 8: Studying Sharks

Shark scientists try to learn all sorts of things about sharks, such as where they live, what they eat, how long they live, and how fast they grow. But did you ever wonder how they study sharks? Let's find out!

## Tag, You're It!

Some sharks are tagged with metal or plastic tags that have a number on them. Scientists capture sharks, measure and weigh them, and then tag and release them. When these

*Caribbean reef shark with a tag*

sharks are seen again by divers, fishermen, or scientists, they report the tag number and where the shark was seen. This helps scientists track where sharks travel and how long they live.

*shark tag*

## Tags that Pop and Ping

Some scientists use tags called "pop-up" tags. These tags give off "pinging" signals that can be followed and mapped. From these tags, scientists can learn where and how far sharks travel. The tags only go for a short ride, though. A few days after being attached, they pop off and float away.

**CLOWNING AROUND!**

**Q:** What do sharks eat with peanut butter?

**A:** Jellyfish!

# Dive, Dive!

Sometimes, scientists dive with sharks to watch them underwater. They can see how sharks swim or hunt, and they sometimes attach tags or take measurements.

*divers with black-tip sharks*

*divers in a cage observing a Galápagos shark*

People who want to watch or film more dangerous sharks, such as great white sharks, stay safe in special metal cages.

# Helping Sharks

Scientists try to help sharks by learning more about them. You can help sharks, too! Here are some ways:

- Learn all you can about sharks. Read about them, visit them at aquariums, and then share what you learn with your friends! Remember: Sharks are cool, not cruel!

- Don't buy sharks' teeth or skin, unless you can be sure that sharks weren't killed just to provide people with souvenirs.

- Help keep the ocean pollution free. All undersea creatures—including sharks—need a healthy, clean ocean to survive.

# What's for Lunch?

It's a bit gross, but scientists like to see what sharks eat. They do this by looking inside a shark's stomach. When fishermen catch a shark, or when they wash up on shore, scientists cut open a shark's tummy to see what they've been eating.

We'll meet a shark scientist in a moment, but first, let's swim over to the next page for some Fishy Fun!

# FISHY FUN: Hide-and-Seek in the Coral Reef

What a lonely coral reef this is! Where are all the fish? Bruce, Chum, and Anchor said that they have 6 different shark friends hanging out around here—but I can't find them. Maybe they're hiding somewhere in the coral and rocks. Take a close look and see if you can find all 6 hidden sharks! *(When you think you've found them all, turn to page 38.)*

# SHOW·AND·TELL

## with Ichthyology Professor, Dr. Gregor Cailliet

Meet Dr. Gregor Cailliet—he's a super shark expert and the Director of the Pacific Shark Research Center at Moss Landing Marine Laboratories in California. Dr. Cailliet is also an ichthyology professor (a teacher who specializes in fishes) and studies all different kinds of sharks and rays. Let's dive into some undersea adventures with him!

### How did you become interested in studying sharks?

**DR. CAILLIET:** I've been interested in fish since I was 12 years old. I spent a lot of time at the beach swimming and surfing. When there were no waves, I would snorkel below the surface and see what lived there. So, I was always curious about all the different creatures living in the sea.

### How do you study sharks?

**DR. CAILLIET:** Most of our studies involve counting the growth bands found in the backbones of sharks. That is how we figure out their age (one pair of growth bands usually equals one year). I also look closely at the other parts of sharks, like their stomachs, to see what they've been eating.

### What kinds of sharks do you study?

**DR. CAILLIET:** I have mostly studied coastal sharks and rays, including leopard and smooth hound sharks, bat rays, angel sharks, and different kinds of stingrays. Recently, I've been concentrating on

leopard shark

fishes that live near the bottom of the ocean—like different kinds of skates.

smooth hound shark

### In your work, what are you trying to learn about sharks?

**DR. CAILLIET:** I'm trying to learn more about their life histories—which includes understanding their growth, how they have babies, and what they eat.

### I've heard that some sharks are in danger. How does this happen?

**DR. CAILLIET:** Sharks and rays are sometimes in danger because they don't grow or have babies fast enough. They're also threatened by the fishing industry. When fishermen catch too many sharks, there are fewer sharks in the ocean that can have babies.

### What do you like most about the work you do?

**DR. CAILLIET:** I like being a professor and a biologist because I get to learn new things every day. And then I get to teach my students what I have learned and help advise them on the research they're doing. I also get to write about my discoveries in books and scientific journals.

# School's Out!

We've finished our swim with the sharks! It was a fun and fascinating ride, wasn't it? You learned that sharks have super-sized senses, that sharks can have live babies just like mammals do, and that sharks aren't really as harmful to people as you might have thought. Sharks are just powerful predators—that's their role in the sea. (You also met the very cool, very large whale shark and found out that it survives by eating some of the smallest things in the ocean!)

Thanks for coming on this ride. This Undersea School class is out for today, but there's a lot more to come. We'll see you next time when we explore some more awesome ocean wonders!

Leaving already? Wouldn't you like to stay for dinner?

Chum! What are you saying?

Don't forget…fish and people are friends, not food!

**Fishy Fun:**
*Searching for Sharks*
*(page 19)*
Did you find all the
shark names?
Let's see where
they were...

| H | C | R | C | T | I | G | E | R | K | E | T |
| O | T | B | C | A | B | S | W | M | E | E | B |
| B | T | U | A | R | R | A | T | B | W | H | A |
| E | O | L | R | R | E | P | M | D | H | P | D |
| N | O | L | P | E | I | L | E | B | T | B | E |
| T | C | H | H | A | P | S | S | C | T | O | C |
| E | R | E | A | P | S | E | A | D | W | T | R |
| E | O | A | L | M | E | A | D | W | N | O | L |
| P | C | D | R | G | U | B | S | S | W | E | L |
| R | O | A | N | I | L | D | E | B | L | I | L |
| R | D | A | F | I | N | E | T | O | O | T | H |
| C | I | S | G | U | L | P | E | R | W | T | M |
| K | L | G | U | K | P | E | A | A | N | O | P |
| L | E | A | N | G | E | L | S | R | L | A | T |
| Y | C | K | L | A | N | T | E | R | N | E | B |
| M | H | S | L | E | E | P | E | R | R | C | A |
| E | M | R | W | D | E | I | R | C | B | B | R |

**Fishy Fun:**
*Hide-and-Seek in the*
*Coral Reef (page 35)*
Where were all those
sharks hiding?
Let's find out!